TREASURY OF LITERATURE

TAKE-HOME BOOKS

VOLUME 1

TO ACCOMPANY
WHISPER A SONG
JUMP RIGHT IN
AND COLOR THE SKY

HARCOURT BRACE & COMPANY

Orlando Atlanta Austin Boston San Francisco Chicago Dallas New York
Toronto London

ISBN 0-15-303597-8

12 13   082   2000 99 98

C O N T E N T S

TAKE-HOME BOOK
WHISPER A SONG

Use with "I Went Walking."

Lion's Walk

by Effie McGee

HARCOURT BRACE & COMPANY

Lion went walking.
He went to see Red Cat.

Come and play, Red Cat.
Can you come and play?
I do not see Red Cat.
I will go to see Green Duck.

Lion! Lion!
Do not be sad.
Green Duck will not run from you.
Brown Cow will not run from you.
And I will not run from you.
Come and play.

2

Red Cat saw Lion walking.
Red Cat went to Green Duck.

Come and play, Brown Cow.
Can you come and play?
I do not see Brown Cow.
I am sad.

7

Green Duck! Green Duck!

Run to the log!

Lion will not see you.

Lion will not see me.

Go in! Go in!

Brown Cow! Brown Cow!

Go in! Go in!

Lion will not see you.

Lion will not see Red Cat.

And Lion will not see me!

I see a lot of ducks.
Come and play, Green Duck.
Can you come and play?
I do not see Green Duck.
I will go to see Brown Cow.

Red Cat and Green Duck saw Lion
walking.
Red Cat and Green Duck went to
Brown Cow.

TAKE-HOME BOOK
JUMP RIGHT IN
Use with "I Wish I Could Fly."

A Nap for Pig

by Marie Richards

HARCOURT BRACE & COMPANY

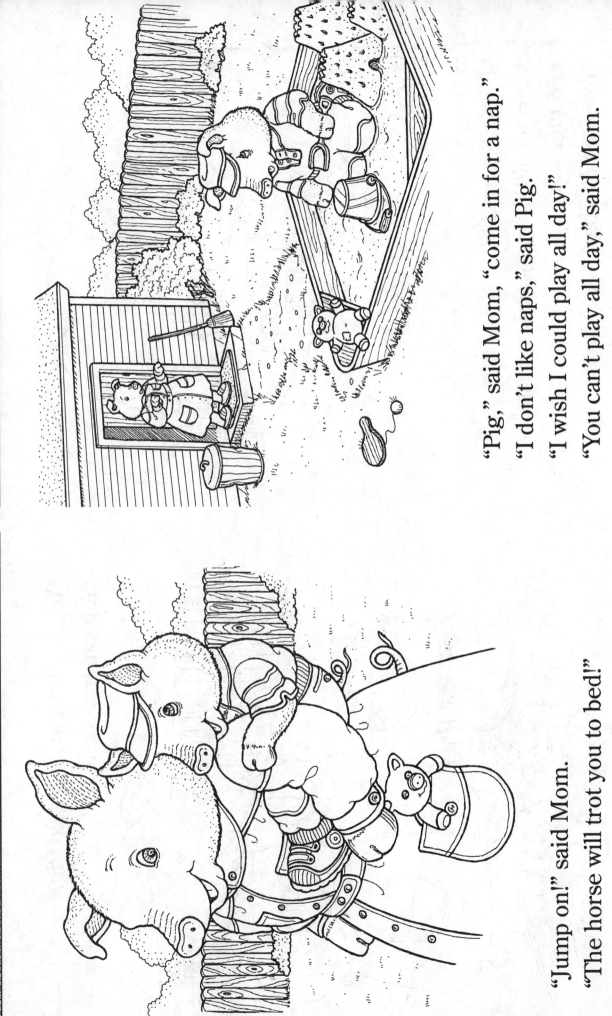

"Pig," said Mom, "come in for a nap."

"I don't like naps," said Pig.

"I wish I could play all day!"

"You can't play all day," said Mom.

"Jump on!" said Mom.

"The horse will trot you to bed!"

"You can be a horse," said Pig.
"You can trot me to bed."

"I wish I were a bird.
A bird could fly away and not nap,"
said Pig.
"You are not a bird," said Mom.

2

7

"I wish I were a frog.
A frog could get wet and not nap," said Pig.
"You are not a frog," said Mom.

"Yes, I do!" said Mom.
"A horse could TROT you to bed for a nap!"

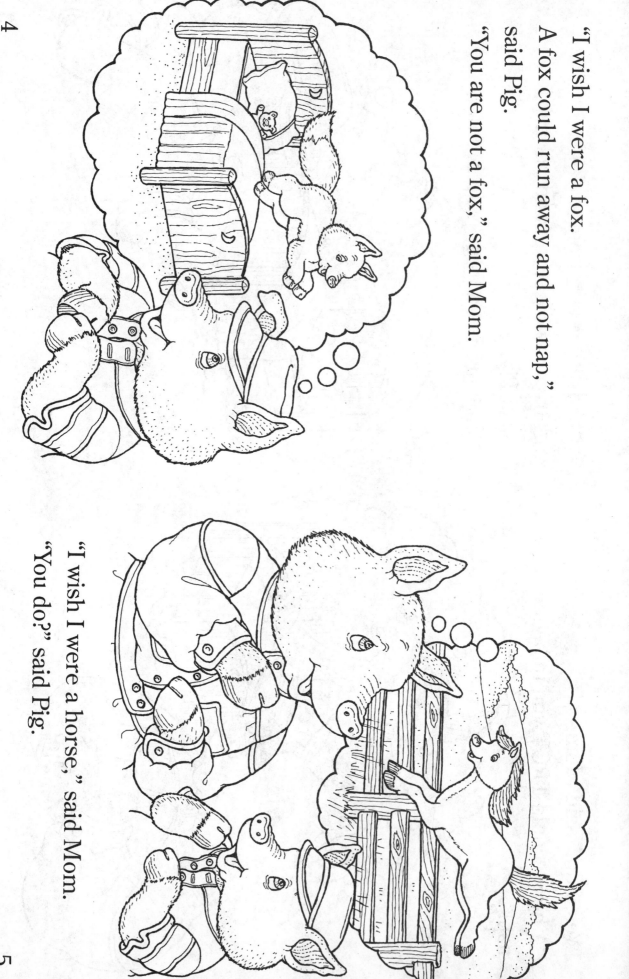

"I wish I were a fox.
A fox could run away and not nap,"
said Pig.
"You are not a fox," said Mom.

4

"I wish I were a horse," said Mom.
"You do?" said Pig.

5

Come and Play

by Marie Richards

TAKE-HOME BOOK
JUMP RIGHT IN
Use with "Six Little Ducks."

HARCOURT BRACE & COMPANY

Little Fox was walking one hot day.

He saw six ducks, I'm happy to say.

And this is why Little Fox came back.

All can play and the ducks can quack.

Over he went and asked to play. "Quack, quack," said the ducks, but they walked away.

Little Fox came down one hot day. He looked and saw, I'm happy to say.

Little Fox was walking one hot day.

He saw four pigs, I'm happy to say.

Over he went and asked to play.

"Yes, yes," said the pigs,
but they went away.

Little Fox looked up on this hot day.

He saw a bird, I'm happy to say.

The little bird said, "Come with me.
We all can play. You will see."

Little Fox was walking one hot day.
He saw one frog, I'm happy to say.

Over he went and asked to play.
"No, no," said Mother Frog,
and she jumped away.

Little Fox was sad one hot day.
"The ducks, pigs, and frog all
ran away.

No one is happy to play with me,
so I will sit up in this green tree."

TAKE-HOME BOOK
JUMP RIGHT IN
Use with "The Chick and the Duckling."

My Chick

by Richard Christopher

HARCOURT BRACE & COMPANY

Jill and Pam went swimming.

"I can swim on this chick," said Jill.

"I can swim on a chick, too,"
said Pam.

"We can make chicks," said Jill.

"Here is my chick."

"Here is my chick, too!" said Pam.

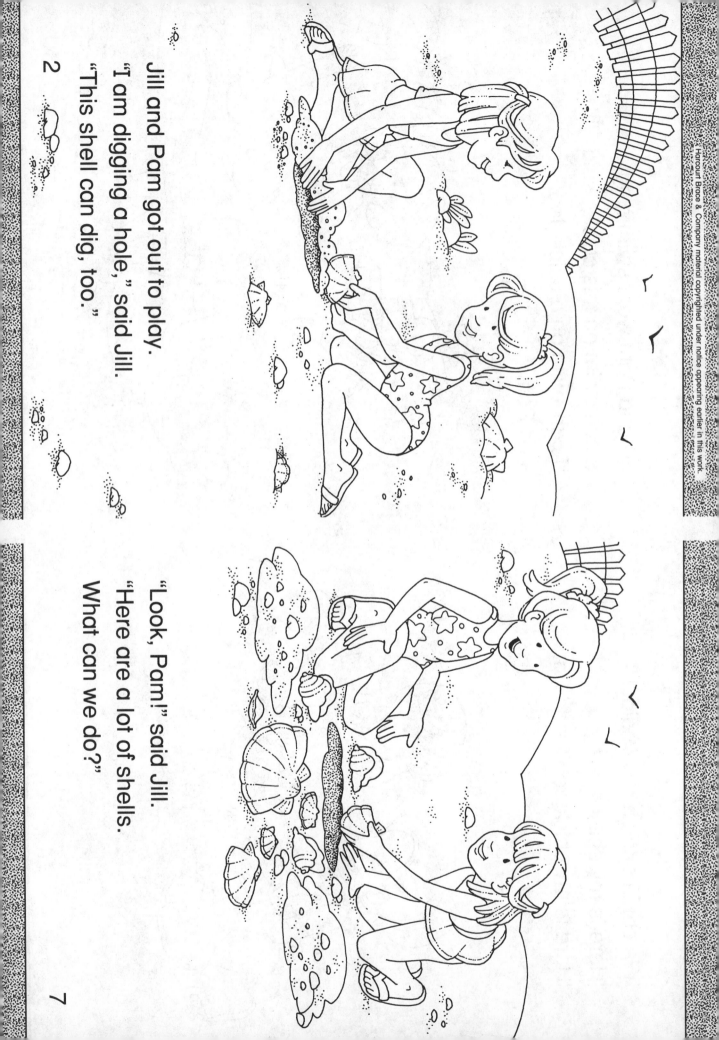

Jill and Pam got out to play.
"I am digging a hole," said Jill.
"This shell can dig, too."

2

"Look, Pam!" said Jill.
"Here are a lot of shells.
What can we do?"

7

"Look! I see a shell," said Pam.

"I will run and get it."

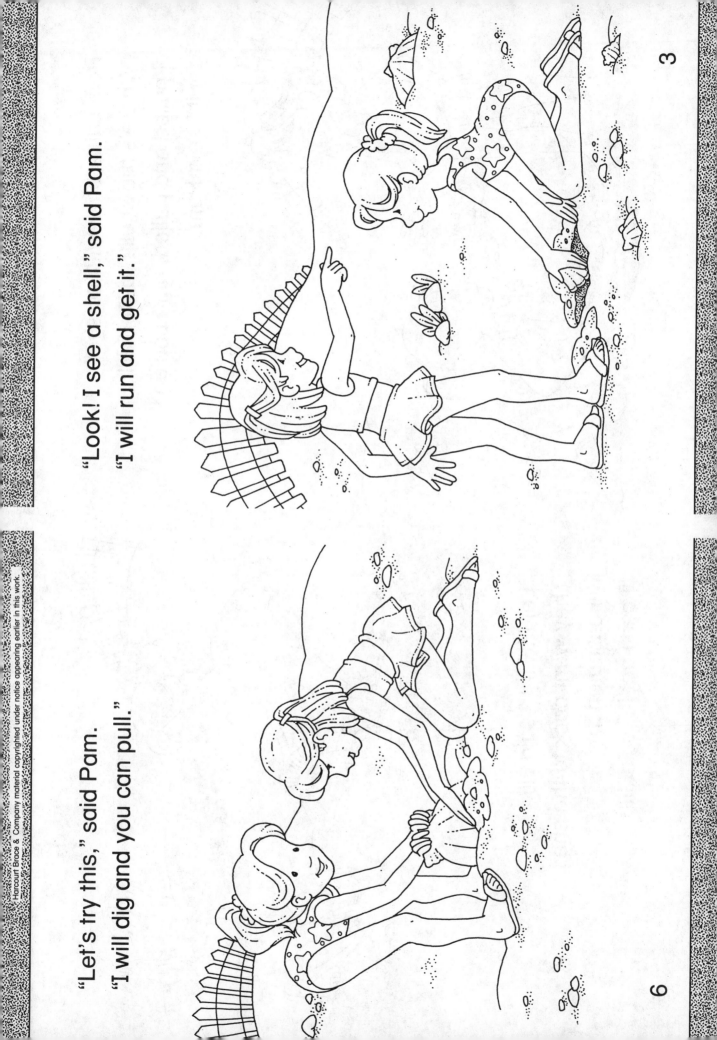

"Let's try this," said Pam.

"I will dig and you can pull."

Pam came back with no shell.

"Where's the shell?" asked Jill.

"I pulled and pulled, but I couldn't get it," said Pam.

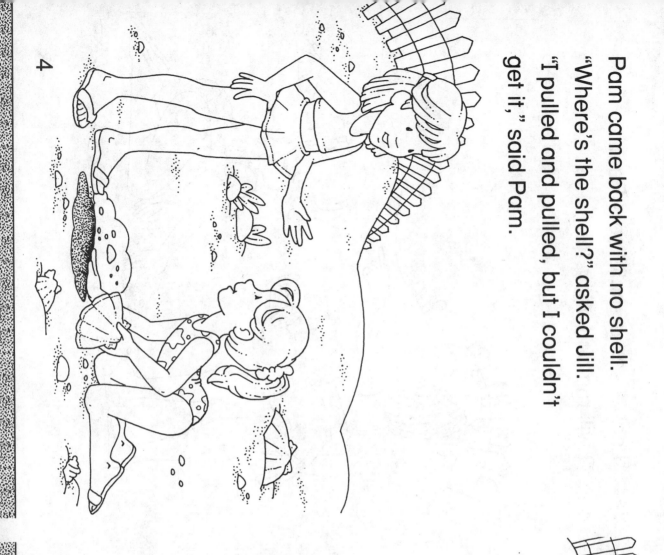

"Let ME try," said Jill.

They went back to the shell.

Jill pulled on it.

"I can't get it," said Jill.

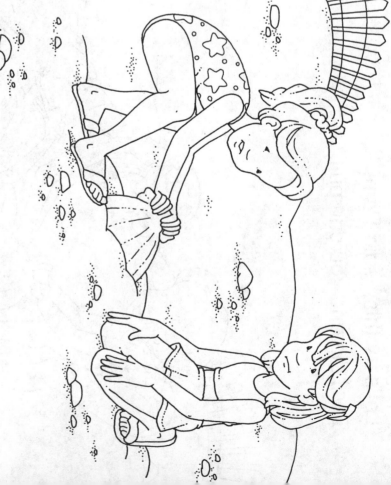

What Do You Wish?

by Tanner Ottley Gay

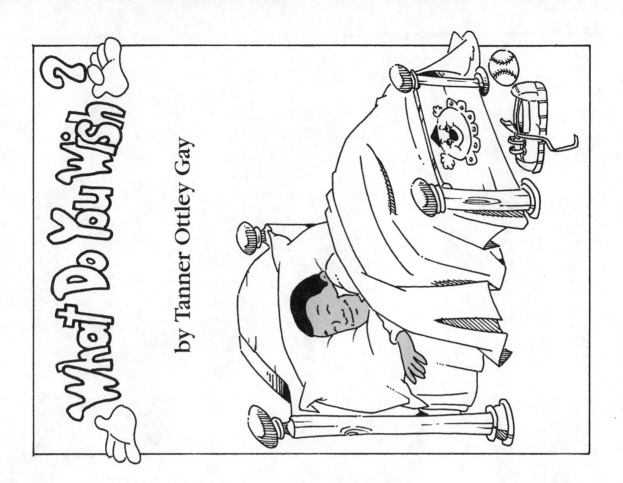

TAKE-HOME BOOK
JUMP RIGHT IN
Use with "Bet You Can't."

HARCOURT BRACE & COMPANY

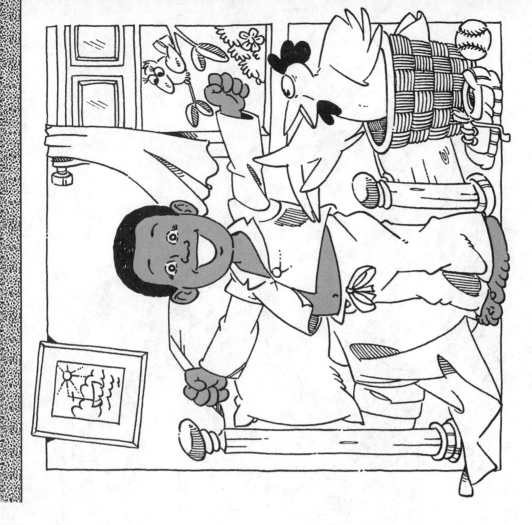

I got up and saw a hen in a basket.

It was a big, red hen.

What a hen it was!

"I'm going back to bed," I said.

"Can you get in the basket and come back, too?"

"No," said the hen. "I have to go."

In the morning, I saw the basket but not the hen.

What did I wish?

I wished for a big, red hen!

The hen said, "Come for a walk.
You can have what you wish."
I went with the hen.

2

"I bet we can get on the horses,"
I said.

"You get on this one. I will lift
you up!"

"What do you wish?" asked the hen.
"I wish my horse could run," I said.
Well, my horse ran and ran!

7

We fell down a big hole.

"What is your wish?" the hen asked.

"I wish I could fly," I said.

"Then you can fly!" said the hen.

Well, the hen and I did fly!

3

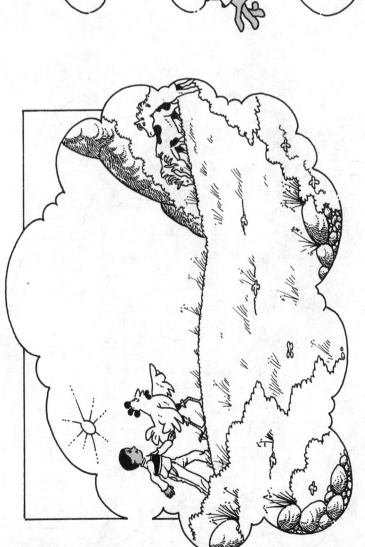

We did swim and swim.

Then we got out.

The hen and I walked and walked.

"We can go over here," said the hen.

6

Then the hen and I walked and walked.

"We can go over here," said the hen.

"It looks clean. Can you jump?"

We jumped, and down we went.

4

"What do you wish?" asked the hen.

"I wish I could swim," I said.

"Then you can swim!" said the hen.

Well, the hen and I did swim.

We did NOT get out!

5

HAM AND CHEESE

© BY CARL PESKE ©

HARCOURT BRACE & COMPANY

"Let's go out for a day," said Cat.
"Yes, let's get out of the house," said Dog.
"What will we bring?"
"What can we dream up?"

"We are all set!" said Dog.
"Here we go!" said Cat.

"I'll bring cheese," said Cat.

"I don't like cheese," said Dog.

"I'll bring ham."

"I don't like ham," said Cat.

"Then I'll make ham and cheese for our day out," said Dog.

"Will you toss me the cheese, Cat?"

"Here, catch!" said Cat.

"If you'll try the ham, I'll try the cheese," said Dog.

"If you'll try the cheese, I'll try the ham," said Cat.

"We can try the ham and cheese together," said Cat.

"I like cheese AND ham," said Cat.

"I like ham AND cheese," said Dog.

So Dog put cheese on the ham.
And Cat put ham on the cheese.

4

"Mmm," said Dog.
"Mmm," said Cat.

5

TAKE-HOME BOOK
COLOR THE SKY
Use with "Five Little Monkeys Jumping on the Bed."

You Can't Trick Mother Hen

by Leigh Rennat

HARCOURT BRACE & COMPANY

One day, Fox went walking. Fox was happy to see Mother Hen and her five little chicks.

Fox walked off.

Mother Hen said to her five little chicks, "You are good little chicks. Fox can not trick me. Fox can not trick my good little chicks!"

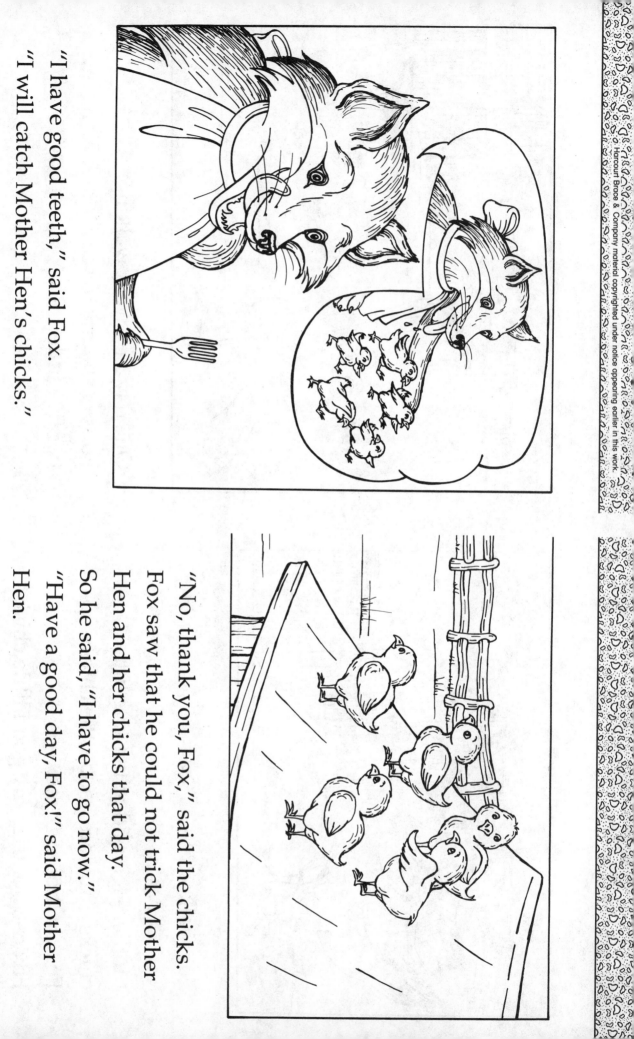

"I have good teeth," said Fox.
"I will catch Mother Hen's chicks."

2

"No, thank you, Fox," said the chicks.
Fox saw that he could not trick Mother
Hen and her chicks that day.
So he said, "I have to go now."
"Have a good day, Fox!" said Mother
Hen.

7

Mother Hen took one look at Fox and
said, "That Fox is up to no good!
Go up on top now, little ones.
Off you go!"

Mother Hen did not let Fox trick her.
"No, Fox," she said. "You can see my
chicks where they are now!"
"Little chicks," said Fox. "Come down
here and play!"

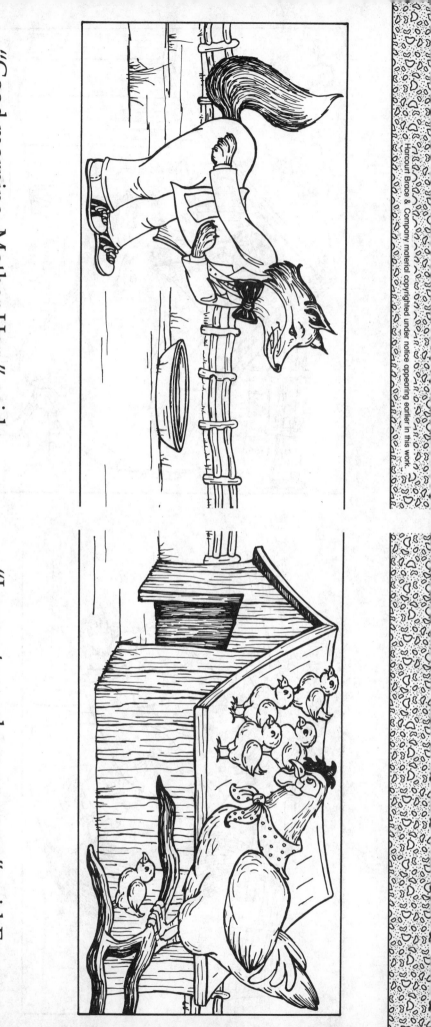

"Good morning, Mother Hen," said Fox.

"Good morning, Fox," said Mother Hen.

"What brings you here?"

"I came to see how you are," said Fox.

"What good-looking chicks you have!"

"Thank you, Fox," said Mother Hen.

"I wish I could see more of them," said Fox.

"Can the chicks come down here?"

4

5

Scamper Today

by William Lakin

TAKE-HOME BOOK
COLOR THE SKY
Use with "Whose Baby?"

HARCOURT BRACE & COMPANY

It was six in the morning.

Sam was not asleep.

He was wide awake.

Sam saw Dog and his pup,

Lion and her cub, Cow and her calf,

and Father Pig and Mother Pig.

He was happy now!

"This IS a good day," said Sam.

"This day belongs to you," said

Father Pig.

Do YOU know what day this is

for Sam?

"Why are you wide awake?" asked Mother Pig.

"This is going to be a good day," said Sam.

"I want to play."

"Why don't you and Father Pig go out and play?" asked Mother Pig.

2

"Come on, Sam," said Father Pig. "We will see where they are going!"

7

Father Pig and Sam played catch.

They saw Dog and his pup.

"Where are you going so fast?"
asked Sam.

Dog and his pup did not say.

"We have to run," said the pup.

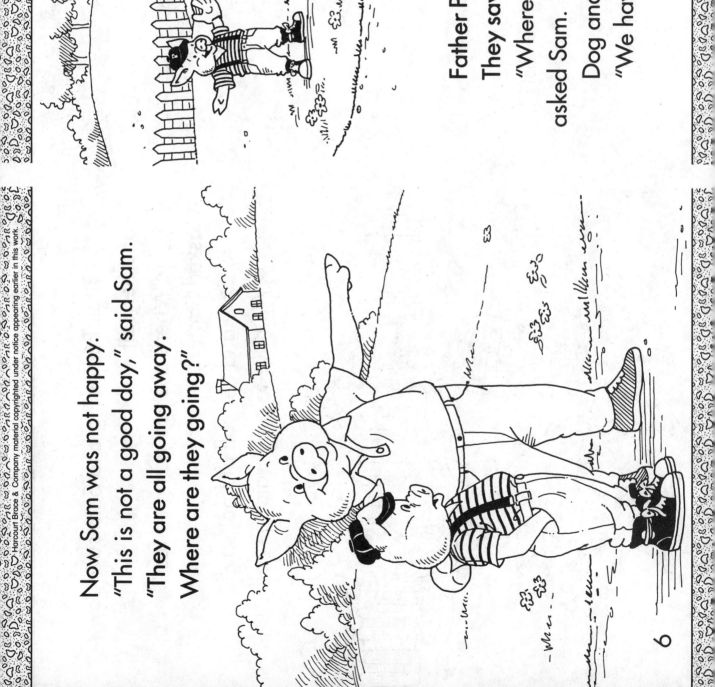

Now Sam was not happy.

"This is not a good day," said Sam.

"They are all going away.

Where are they going?"

Then Father Pig and Sam saw Lion and her cub.

"Where are you going so fast?" asked Sam.

Lion and her cub did not say.

"We have to run," said the cub.

4

Then Father Pig and Sam saw Cow and her calf.

"Where are you going so fast?" asked Sam.

Cow and her calf did not say.

"We have to run," said the calf.

5

Best Friends

by Tanner Ottley Gay

TAKE-HOME BOOK
COLOR THE SKY
Use with "My Best Friend."

HARCOURT BRACE & COMPANY

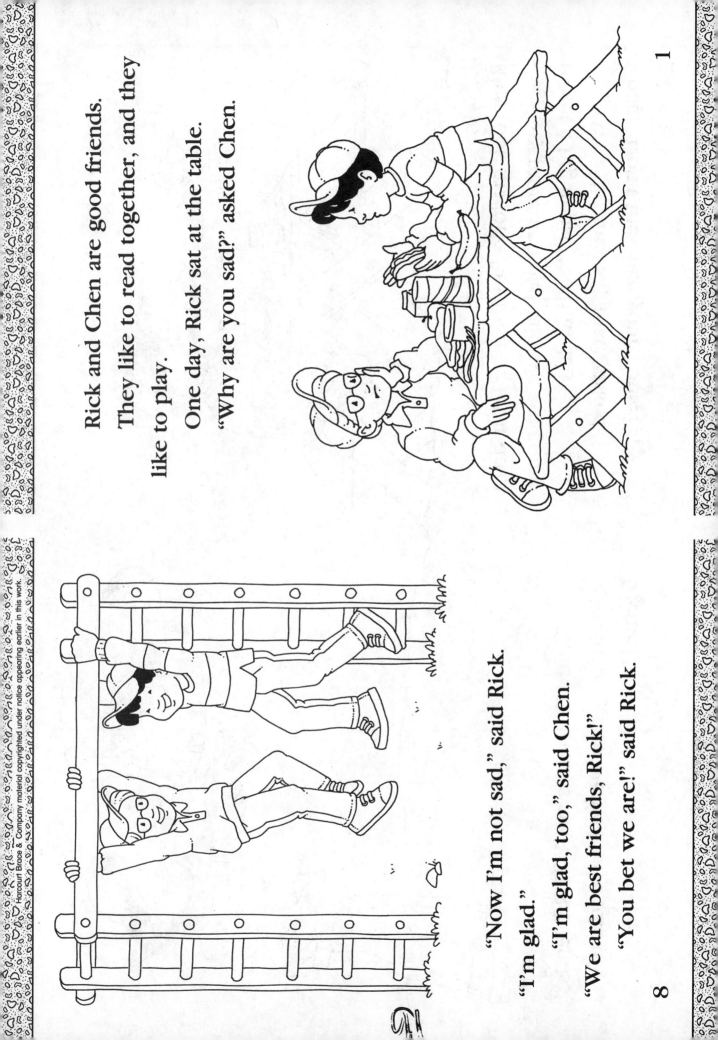

Rick and Chen are good friends.

They like to read together, and they like to play.

One day, Rick sat at the table.

"Why are you sad?" asked Chen.

1

"Now I'm not sad," said Rick.

"I'm glad."

"I'm glad, too," said Chen.

"We are best friends, Rick!"

"You bet we are!" said Rick.

8

Rick took his fork. But then he let it drop.

"My mom and dad said we are going to get a big house," said Rick.

"Why did they say that?" asked Chen. "Don't they like your house?"

2

"And MY friends are YOUR friends," said Chen. "Then we will have lots of friends!"

7

"Our house is not big," said Rick.

"With the baby, we will not all fit

in our house."

"Where will you go?" asked Chen.

"We will go to a house that is bigger

than our house is," said Rick.

3

"We can make friends, too," said

Rick.

"Then MY friends are YOUR

friends."

6

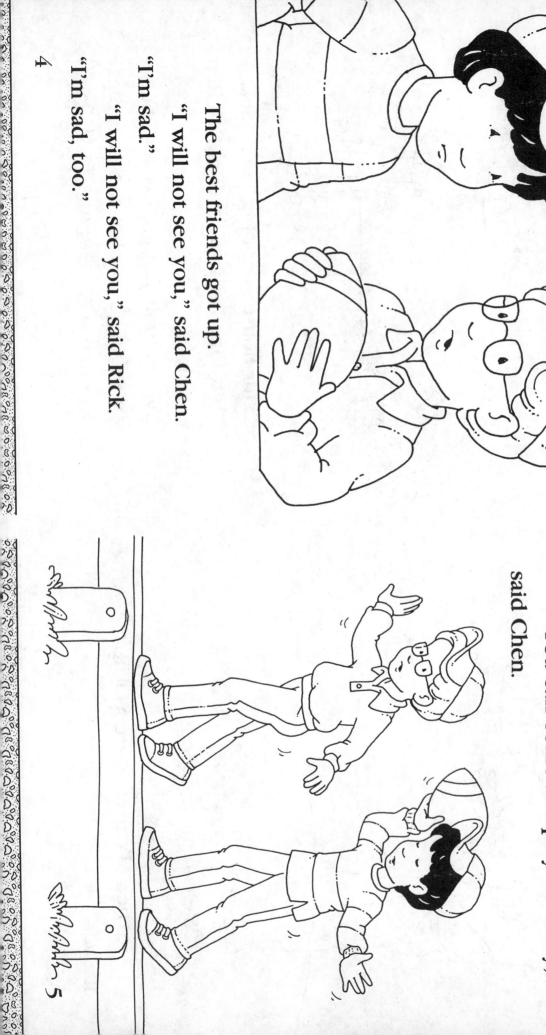

The best friends got up.
"I will not see you," said Chen.
"I'm sad."
"I will not see you," said Rick.
"I'm sad, too."

4

"You can come and play for a day,"
said Rick.
"You can come and play for a day,"
said Chen.

5

Bike Day

by Patricia Ann Becker

TAKE-HOME BOOK
COLOR THE SKY
Use with "How Joe the Bear and Sam the Mouse Got Together."

HARCOURT BRACE & COMPANY

This is my bike and I love to ride it.

My bike is not like your bike.

My bike is like a friend.

We all went down the walk together.

More friends came out with bikes.

Now everyone can see that today is Bike Day.

You can have a Bike Day, too!

HOORAY FOR BIKES

BIKE DAY

One day my bike said, "Today is not Mother's Day or Father's Day. Today is Bike Day!"

"What's Bike Day?" I asked.

"Hit the top like this," I said.

Then my friends came out.

"What's going on?" they asked.

"Today is Bike Day," I said.

"Go get your bikes. We can all play together."

"Bike Day is a day to be kind to your bike," my bike said.

"On Bike Day you try to make your bike happy!"

"Now lets play together," I said.

"I'll ring my bell for you," my bike said.

"I'll play my drum for you," I said to my bike.

"I cannot play the drum."

"How do you play it?" asked my bike.

"I can do that," I said.
"Every day I ride on you.
Today I will give you a ride to
a place you want to go. Hop in!"
"This is fun," said my bike.
"Thanks for the ride!"

"Now we can eat," I said.
"Do you like to eat?"
"I love to eat," my bike said.
"Then try this," I said.
"This is good," said my bike.
"Thank you!"

TAKE-HOME BOOK
COLOR THE SKY
Use with "Mouse Tales."

A House for Mouse

by Mary Clark

HARCOURT BRACE & COMPANY

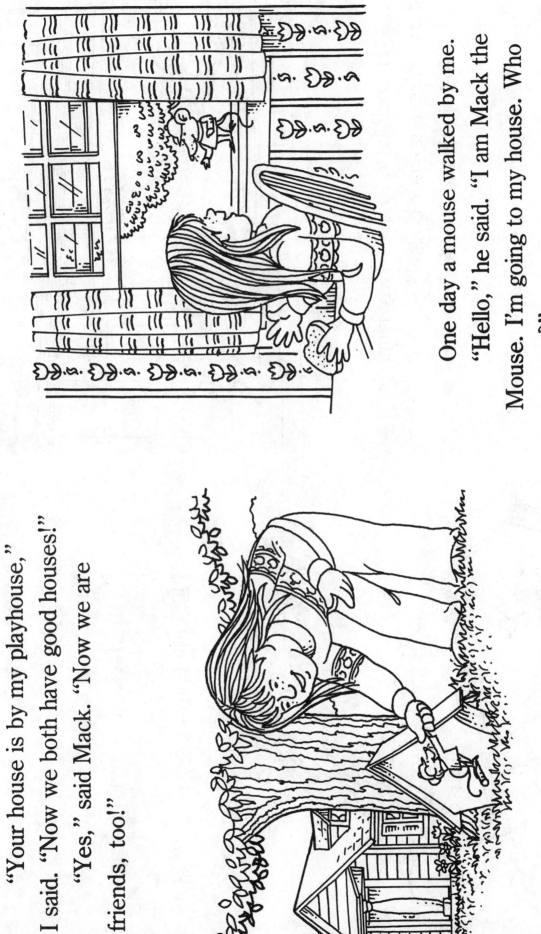

"Your house is by my playhouse," I said. "Now we both have good houses!"

"Yes," said Mack. "Now we are friends, too!"

One day a mouse walked by me. "Hello," he said. "I am Mack the Mouse. I'm going to my house. Who are you?"

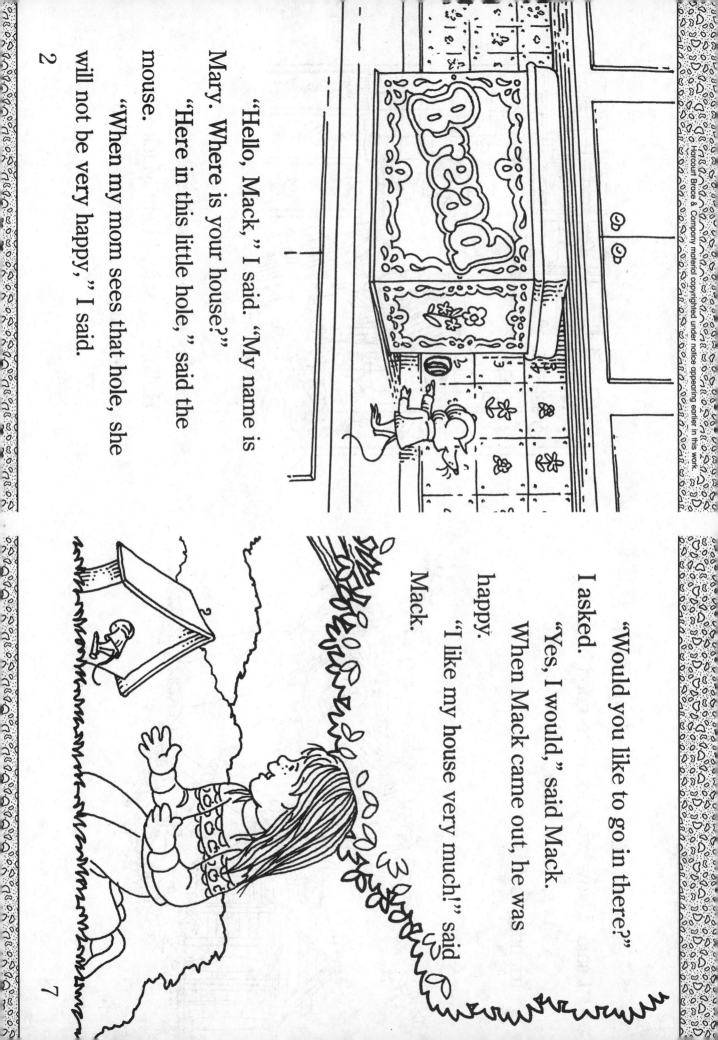

"Hello, Mack," I said. "My name is Mary. Where is your house?"

"Here in this little hole," said the mouse.

"When my mom sees that hole, she will not be very happy," I said.

2

"Would you like to go in there?" I asked.

"Yes, I would," said Mack. When Mack came out, he was happy.

"I like my house very much!" said Mack.

7

"I am very happy in this house," said the mouse.

"I can take you to a good house," I said. "You would like the house very much."

"There is your house," I said.

"Is this a birdhouse?" asked Mack.

"No. It WAS a birdhouse," I said.

"But it fell from the tree. Now it is a mouse house."

"When can you take me there,
Mary?" asked Mack the Mouse. "Can
we go there soon?"

"Yes," I said. "I will take you there
now!"

© Harcourt Brace & Company material copyrighted under notice appearing earlier in this work.

"I would like a good house," said
Mack. "I will go and pack."

Soon he came back with a little bag.
We both walked out of the house
together.